The Healing Path

Using the Stations of the Cross
to Heal from Childhood Sexual Abuse

ISBN: 978-0-615-59465-1
Copyright 2012 by J. M. Mitchell
Schenectady, NY: Feather Press

The Stations of the Cross used in this text are taken from
this source:

The Book of Occasional Services (2003 ed.). New York,
NY: Church Publishing

The icons of the Stations of the Cross included in this text
were photographed on location by the author at the
following address:

Community of St. Mary, Eastern Province
242 Cloister Way
Greenwich, NY 12834

Table of Contents

Introduction

In 2011, a meta-analysis of 217 studies from around the world revealed the most current estimates of the prevalence of childhood sexual abuse[1]. The studies included in the analysis spanned 28 years, from 1980 to 2008, and included data from 9,911,748 participants. Worldwide, 127 children out of every 1000 reported that they had experienced childhood sexual abuse. Although more girls than boys reported experiencing childhood sexual abuse (180 girls out of every 1000), boys are significantly affected, and 76 boys out of every 1000 reported experiencing childhood sexual abuse. Although many childhood sexual abuse survivors feel alone in their experiences, childhood sexual abuse touches so many lives that in all likelihood they have met other survivors without even realizing it.

Childhood sexual abuse exacts a cost from survivors. If the damage were only physical the help of health professionals would be all that was necessary to heal from the abuse, but there are spiritual consequences as well. By and large, childhood sexual abuse survivors express anger at God for permitting the abuse to occur, and experience an estrangement from God that can endure far past the childhood years. This devotional is meant to address faulty beliefs that perpetuate this estrangement and assist survivors in restoring their relationship with God.

Each Station of the Cross is accompanied by a Reflection with suggestions intended to promote healing. It is suggested that the reader invest in a rosary and at the

---

[1] Stoltenborgh, M., van IJzendoorn, M. H., Euser, E. M., Bakermans Kranenburg, M. J. (2011). A global perspective on child sexual abuse: Meta-analysis of prevalence around the world. Child Maltreatment, 16(2):79-101

end of each Station recite the prayer "Holy God, Holy and Mighty, Holy Immortal One, Have mercy upon us." or another prayer that won't be too distracting several times while reflecting on the image provided of the Station before moving on to the Reflection.

You may choose to use this guide when praying the Stations of the Cross in your own church or at a shrine. Pilgrimage can be good for the soul, and the artistic renderings of the Stations are so diverse that one may glean unique insights by studying the Stations of the Cross wherever they are found.

This devotional is meant to be used in conjunction with traditional psychotherapy, therapeutic groups for sexual abuse survivors, Theophostic prayer ministry, and other books on childhood sexual abuse. You may find it helpful to keep a journal while working through this text so you can write down any important insights as they emerge. As with any devotional you will get as much out of this text as you put into it. The Stations are meant to be worked slowly and in order, so don't be surprised if you spend a month or more working through each Station the first time through. The suggested research in Stations 4-7 in particular will take time, and it may take even more time to get in touch with your memories of the abuse. Trust God's timeline for your healing and be gentle with yourself.

The Cross

Opening Devotions

In the Name of the Father, and of the Son, and of the Holy
Spirit. Amen.

Lord, have mercy.
Christ, have mercy.
Lord, have mercy.

Our Father, who art in heaven,
hallowed be thy Name,
thy kingdom come,
thy will be done,
on earth as it is in heaven.
Give us this day our daily bread.
And forgive us our trespasses,
as we forgive those
who trespass against us.
And lead us not into temptation,
but deliver us from evil.

V. We will glory in the cross of our Lord Jesus Christ:
R. In whom is our salvation, our life and resurrection.

Let us pray. (Silence)

Assist us mercifully with your help, O Lord God of our
salvation, that we may enter with joy upon the
contemplation of those mighty acts, whereby you have
given us life and immortality; through Jesus Christ our
Lord. Amen.

The procession goes to the First Station.

Reflection

Jesus came that we might have life, and have it abundantly (John 10:10). But if childhood sexual abuse has touched our life we may find it difficult to embrace all that a life in Christ has to offer. The Psalms tell us that God is able to heal the brokenhearted and bind up their wounds (Psalm 147:3), but many survivors are reluctant to ask God for healing. We forget that God, in the person of Jesus, has an intimate knowledge of our human suffering and can provide valuable support.

As you prepare to meditate upon the Stations of the Cross open your heart to Jesus and ask him to bind up your wounds. Ask Jesus to reveal his humanity to you as you reflect upon the Stations, and in return, be willing to share your humanity with him: share your thoughts, feelings, and physical responses. As much as possible, don't censor yourself. Let the Stations become an honest dialogue between you and Jesus.

Express gratitude that the Holy Spirit has prompted you to reexamine your childhood at this point in your life and be open to seeing how the suffering Jesus endured during his passion was similar to the suffering you endured during your abuse.

I

First Station

Jesus is condemned to death

We adore you, O Christ, and we bless you:
Because by your holy cross you have redeemed the world.

As soon as it was morning, the chief priests, with the elders and scribes, and the whole council, held a consultation; and they bound Jesus and led him away and delivered him to Pilate. And they all condemned him and said, "He deserves to die." When Pilate heard these words, he brought Jesus out and sat down on the judgment seat at a place called the Pavement, but in the Hebrew, Gabbatha. Then he handed Jesus over to them to be crucified.

V. God did not spare his own Son:
R. But delivered him up for us all.

Let us pray. (Silence)

Almighty God, whose most dear Son went not up to joy but first he suffered pain, and entered not into glory before he was crucified: Mercifully grant that we, walking in the way of the cross, may find it none other than the way of life and peace; through Jesus Christ your Son our Lord. Amen.

Holy God,
Holy and Mighty,
Holy Immortal One,
Have mercy upon us.

Reflection

If we embrace the promise of Christ that we will have life in abundance there may come a point when our life circumstances invite us to examine our childhoods for the beliefs that have kept that promise from coming true. The beliefs we form in childhood are shaped by circumstance and our change of circumstance in adulthood provides us with the opportunity to revisit the time when our beliefs were formed and ask ourselves whether we still consider them to be true.

As you meditate upon the Stations, you will be reevaluating your childhood beliefs and determining whether they are still true. Currently, you are like Pilate, attempting to render a judgment regarding the case that has been brought before you. And although it is indeed a child of God who is before you, it is your childhood self rather than Jesus. Take the investigation seriously. Just as Pilate's decision to have Jesus crucified impacted Jesus' life and the lives of many other people, your decision to examine your childhood beliefs will impact your life and the lives of others.

II

Second Station

Jesus takes up his Cross.

We adore you, O Christ, and we bless you:
Because by your holy cross you have redeemed the world.

Jesus went out, bearing his own cross, to the place called
the place of a skull, which is called in Hebrew, Golgotha.
Although he was a Son, he learned obedience through what
he suffered. Like a lamb he was led to the slaughter; and
like a sheep that before its shearers is mute, so he opened
not his mouth. Worthy is the Lamb who was slain, to
receive power and riches and wisdom and strength and
honor and glory and blessing.

V. The Lord has laid on him the iniquity of us all:
R. For the transgression of my people was he stricken.

Let us pray. (Silence)

Almighty God, whose beloved Son willingly endured the
agony and shame of the cross for our redemption: Give us
courage to take up our cross and follow him; who lives and
reigns for ever and ever. Amen.

Holy God,
Holy and Mighty,
Holy Immortal One,
Have mercy upon us.

Reflection

For some abuse survivors, accepting the experience of childhood sexual abuse may only happen after years of denial. The loss of an addiction, a significant relationship, or a life goal prompts us to consider whether we were abused, and for some, a flooding of painful memories ensues.

We learn the truth, and although it may initially feel like that truth may kill us, that truth is the very thing that can set us free. In the past, when our actions were guided by subconscious fears and erroneous beliefs, when we used addictive substances or behaviors to repress painful memories, we were not living freely. By accepting the truth that you were sexually abused as a child you are picking up your cross and taking responsibility for your healing process.

III

Third Station

Jesus falls the first time

We adore you, O Christ, and we bless you:
Because by your holy cross you have redeemed the world.

Christ Jesus, though he was in the form of God, did not count equality with God a thing to be grasped; but emptied himself, taking the form of a servant, and was born in human likeness. And being found in human form he humbled himself and became obedient unto death, even death on a cross. Therefore God has highly exalted him, and bestowed on him the name which is above every name. Come, let us bow down, and bend the knee, and kneel before the Lord our Maker, for he is the Lord our God.

V. Surely he has borne our griefs:
R. And carried our sorrows.

Let us pray. *(Silence)*

O God, you know us to be set in the midst of so many and great dangers, that by reason of the frailty of our nature we cannot always stand upright: Grant us such strength and protection as may support us in all dangers, and carry us through all temptations; through Jesus Christ our Lord. *Amen.*

Holy God,
Holy and Mighty,
Holy Immortal One,
Have mercy upon us.

Reflection

Having accepted the reality that you were sexually abused as a child you can now give your full attention to the task which was assigned to you at the time you were abused: suffering. Though it may surprise you, suffering serves a purpose. It is our God-given ability to suffer which helps us to learn and to grow.

As you meditate upon the Third Station, ask God for the grace to endure the suffering you may experience as you reflect upon your memories so you can complete the reevaluation of your childhood beliefs. It is no mistake that you are on this path, the Holy Spirit prompts us to take those steps which are necessary for us to experience the fullness of our life in Christ. Surrender to the process and know that God is with you.

IV

Fourth Station

Jesus meets his afflicted mother

We adore you, O Christ, and we bless you:
Because by your holy cross you have redeemed the world.

To what can I liken you, to what can I compare you, O daughter of Jerusalem? What likeness can I use to comfort you, O virgin daughter of Zion? For vast as the sea is your ruin. Blessed are those who mourn, for they shall be comforted. The Lord will be your everlasting light, and your days of mourning shall be ended.

V. A sword will pierce your own soul also:
R. And fill your heart with bitter pain.

Let us pray. *(Silence)*

O God, who willed that in the passion of your Son a sword of grief should pierce the soul of the Blessed Virgin Mary his mother: Mercifully grant that your Church, having shared with her in his passion, may be made worthy to share in the joys of his resurrection; who lives and reigns for ever and ever. *Amen.*

Holy God,
Holy and Mighty,
Holy Immortal One,
Have mercy upon us.

Reflection

At the Fourth Station, Jesus meets his afflicted mother. As you reflect upon this Station, try to put yourself in Mary's position and reflect upon the memories of your own abuse from the third person perspective.

Many survivors of childhood sexual abuse report dissociating from themselves during the abuse, and watching the abuse occur from a distant point, in a corner for example, or from the ceiling. Access those memories and observe your childhood self during the abuse. Strive to feel the same compassion for yourself that Mary felt for her Son Jesus.

V

Fifth Station

The Cross is laid on Simon of Cyrene

We adore you, O Christ, and we bless you:
Because by your holy cross you have redeemed the world.

As they led Jesus away, they came upon a man of Cyrene, Simon by name, who was coming in from the country, and laid on him the cross to carry it behind Jesus. "If anyone would come after me, let him deny himself and take up his cross and follow me. Take my yoke upon you, and learn from me; for my yoke is easy, and my burden is light."

V. Whoever does not bear his own cross and come
    after me:
R. Cannot be my disciple.

Let us pray. *(Silence)*

Heavenly Father, whose blessed Son came not to be served but to serve: Bless all who, following in his steps, give themselves to the service of others; that with wisdom, patience and courage, they may minister in his Name to the suffering, the friendless, and the needy; for the love of him who laid down his life for us, your Son our Savior Jesus Christ. *Amen.*

Holy God,
Holy and Mighty,
Holy Immortal One,
Have mercy upon us.

Reflection

At the Fifth Station, Simon of Cyrene share Jesus' burden of carrying the cross. As you reflect upon this Station, take Simon's position and review the memories of your abuse from the second person position.

Though it may be intimidating or fill you with anger or resentment initially, take this opportunity to examine your abuse from the standpoint of your abuser(s). Was your abuser a pedophile or an ephebophile? A serial rapist? What sort? Did s/he suffer from a sexual addiction? Did s/he abuse alcohol or other drugs at the time the abuse was perpetrated? Was s/he sexually abused as a child? How many children did your abuser abuse to your knowledge?

The object of this reflection is to get you to think hypothetically about the possible motives of your abuser(s). Time spent completing this step is time well spent. When you start to feel compassion for your abuser it is time to move on to the Sixth Station.

VI

Sixth Station

A woman wipes the face of Jesus

We adore you, O Christ, and we bless you:
Because by your holy cross you have redeemed the world.

We have seen him without beauty or majesty, with no looks
to attract our eyes. He was despised and rejected by men; a
man of sorrows, and acquainted with grief; and as one from
whom men hide their faces, he was despised, and we
esteemed him not. His appearance was so marred, beyond
human semblance, and his form beyond that of the children
of men. But he was wounded for our transgressions, he was
bruised for our iniquities; upon him was the chastisement
that made us whole, and with his stripes we are healed.

V. Restore us, O Lord God of hosts:
R. Show the light of your countenance, and we shall be
saved.

Let us pray. *(Silence)*

O God, who before the passion of your only-begotten Son
revealed his glory upon the holy mountain: Grant to us that
we, beholding by faith the light of his countenance, may be
strengthened to bear our cross, and be changed into his
likeness from glory to glory; through Jesus Christ our Lord.
Amen.

Holy God,
Holy and Mighty,
Holy Immortal One,
Have mercy upon us.

Reflection

At the Sixth Station, a woman wipes the sweat and blood from Jesus' face to reveal his glorious visage. We are invited in meditating upon this Station to wipe the dust from our recollection of the circumstances surrounding our abuse and attempt to perceive the facts as accurately as possible, thus improving our chances of finding God in our recollection. God is truth (Isaiah 65:16), and if we find the truth we will likely find that God is nearby.

Years of fearful evasion can distort our perception of the abuse. When we confront our fear and seek to see people and events as they truly were at the time of our abuse our perceptions about the abuse may change. Just as your perception of your abuser(s) may have changed as a result of the work you did at the Fifth Station, your perception of the circumstances may change as a result of working the Sixth Station.

What was your household like growing up? Were your parents at home or frequently absent? Did they abuse alcohol or other drugs? Did either parent have a significant physical or mental illness while you were growing up? What sort of a relationship did you have with them prior to the abuse? Did you tell them about the abuse? Why or why not? How did your relationship with members of your family change as a result of the abuse?

You may find it helpful to ask a trusted family member for insight regarding what your childhood home was like from their perspective. Siblings may be the best source for information in this regard. When you can put yourself in the shoes of your childhood self on a typical day when you were likely to be abused you have accomplished your mission.

VII

Seventh Station

Jesus falls a second time

We adore you, O Christ, and we bless you:
Because by your holy cross you have redeemed the world.

Surely he has borne our griefs and carried our sorrows. All we like sheep have gone astray; we have turned every one to his own way; and the Lord has laid on him the iniquity of us all. He was oppressed, and he was afflicted, yet he opened not his mouth. For the transgression of my people was he stricken.

V. But as for me, I am a worm and no man:
R. Scorned by all and despised by the people.

Let us pray. *(Silence)*

Almighty and everliving God, in your tender love for the human race you sent your Son our Savior Jesus Christ to take upon him our nature, and to suffer death upon the cross, giving us the example of his great humility: Mercifully grant that we may walk in the way of his suffering, and also share in his resurrection; who lives and reigns for ever and ever. *Amen.*

Holy God,
Holy and Mighty,
Holy Immortal One,
Have mercy upon us.

Reflection

Now that you have a sense of what life was like at the time you were abused you can start to consider how social factors contributed to your abuse. If one or both of your parents were frequently absent due to work, there were economic forces that contributed to your abuse. If one or both of your parents abused alcohol or other drugs, the force of addiction and policies regarding drug control played a role. If you were performing badly at school as a result of the abuse and your parents were advised to medicate you rather than get to the root of your poor performance, there were political forces in the sphere of educational policy that may have contributed to your suffering. Were either of your parents victims of childhood sexual abuse? We know that sexual abuse tends to be multigenerational in families and many factors play a role in the repetition of the cycle of abuse. Explore how the culture in which you lived at the time of your abuse may have made you susceptible to abuse. Consider how social norms contributed to the duration of the abuse and to the extent to which your abuser was held responsible for his or her behavior. Consider how the paradigm of Western medicine or the availability of medical insurance influenced the kind of treatment you received after the abuse. Pick up an introductory Sociology textbook and get a sense of how your society works. Read books or research articles about multigenerational abuse, alcohol or substance abuse, poverty, or any other variable that you feel may have impacted your circumstances as a child prior to, during, and after the abuse. Strive to get a sense of how social factors influenced your behavior, the behavior of your abuser, your parents' behavior, and the behavior of other third parties including your extended family, teachers, and neighbors.

VIII

Eighth Station

Jesus meets the women of Jerusalem

We adore you, O Christ, and we bless you:
Because by your holy cross you have redeemed the world.

There followed after Jesus a great multitude of the people, and among them were women who bewailed and lamented him. But Jesus turning to them said, "Daughters of Jerusalem, do not weep for me, but weep for yourselves and for your children."

V. Those who sowed with tears:
R. Will reap with songs of joy.

Let us pray. *(Silence)*

Teach your Church, O Lord, to mourn the sins of which it is guilty, and to repent and forsake them; that, by your pardoning grace, the results of our iniquities may not be visited upon our children and our children's children; through Jesus Christ our Lord. *Amen.*

Holy God,
Holy and Mighty,
Holy Immortal One,
Have mercy upon us.

Reflection

Having identified the role that social factors played in your abuse, the Eighth Station provides the opportunity to grieve 'for us and for our children'. Maybe you learned about the role economics played in limiting the amount of supervision your parents provided, and realized that other children (maybe your own?) are also susceptible to abuse for the same reason. Maybe you learned about multigenerational abuse, and a reluctance to confront the reality of your own abuse has blinded you to the sexual abuse of your own child or other children in your life. Maybe growing up in an alcoholic home rendered you indifferent to the serious hazard that buzzed parenting poses to children's safety. Take this time to grieve the social faults that put you and other children at risk of abuse. Part of the healing path is feeling a sense of solidarity with people who behave badly because they are suffering. Working the Seventh and Eighth Stations may inspire greater compassion for those who were involved in your abuse and make you more cognizant of the factors that place children at risk. Be thankful that you can apply your hard-earned knowledge to keep children safe and perhaps even prevent the abuse that you endured from being perpetrated again.

IX

Ninth Station

Jesus falls a third time

We adore you, O Christ, and we bless you:
Because by your holy cross you have redeemed the world.

I am the man who has seen affliction under the rod of his wrath; he has driven and brought me into darkness without any light. He has besieged me and enveloped me with bitterness and tribulation; he has made me dwell in darkness like the dead of long ago. Though I call and cry for help, he shuts out my prayer. He has made my teeth grind on gravel, and made me cower in ashes. "Remember, O Lord, my affliction and bitterness, the wormwood and the gall!"

V. He was led like a lamb to the slaughter:
R. And like a sheep that before its shearers is mute, so he opened not his mouth.

Let us pray. *(Silence)*

O God, by the passion of your blessed Son you made an instrument of shameful death to be for us the means of life: grant us so to glory in the cross of Christ, that we may gladly suffer shame and loss for the sake of your Son our Savior Jesus Christ. *Amen.*

Holy God,
Holy and Mighty,
Holy Immortal One,
Have mercy upon us.

Reflection

Now that you have examined your abuse from the perspective of the third person and second person and have placed the abuse in a cultural perspective, identifying social factors that contributed to your abuse, you are ready to petition God (and possibly a trusted friend) to be with you as you review the memories of your abuse from the first person perspective in prayer.

Remember to maintain a dialogue with God. Ask God to reveal to you where he was at the time of the abuse. Many abuse survivors believe that God abandoned them at the time of their abuse, and fault God for failing to intervene on their behalf. They project their anger for the negligence of parents and others responsible for their welfare at the time of their abuse onto God, when God had entrusted their caregivers with that responsibility. Jesus calls his disciples to love one another as we love ourselves (John 13:34) but not all people choose to follow Christ. We ended up as children in the hands of unbelievers who did to us as they saw fit. Jesus knows our pain. Reflect on those childhood memories again and you may be surprised to find God's presence in the background, and his love shaping the consequences of your abuse in a way that would turn out okay in the end.

X

Tenth Station

Jesus is stripped of his garments

We adore you, O Christ, and we bless you:
Because by your holy cross you have redeemed the world.

When they came to a place called Golgotha (which means
the place of a skull), they offered him wine to drink,
mingled with gall; but when he tasted it, he would not drink
it. And they divided his garments among them by casting
lots. This was to fulfill the scripture which says, "They
divided my garments among them; they cast lots for my
clothing."

V. They gave me gall to eat:
R. And when I was thirsty they gave me vinegar to drink.

Let us pray. *(Silence)*

Lord God, whose blessed Son our Savior gave his body to
be whipped and his face to be spit upon: Give us grace to
accept joyfully the sufferings of the present time, confident
of the glory that shall be revealed; through Jesus Christ our
Lord. *Amen.*

Holy God,
Holy and Mighty,
Holy Immortal One,
Have mercy upon us.

Reflection

For abuse survivors the Tenth Station can be oddly reminiscent of our abuse experiences. Jesus is stripped of his garments. His human dignity is violated. At a time when you may be tempted to retreat from reflecting upon your childhood memories remember that Jesus, when he was offered intoxicants by his abusers, chose to remain sober and endure the humiliation and cruelty of his abuse.

This is your time to retrospectively experience the degradation of your abuse and accept it, letting go of any attempt to control the outcome. The abuse was out of your control, and while your body may have been at the mercy of your abuser, your soul was safe in God's hands. Jesus tells his followers not to fear those who can destroy the body but cannot harm the soul (Matthew 10:28). Find the courage to endure the abuse as you remember it, just as Jesus did, knowing that your soul is your most precious commodity and it was not in jeopardy during the abuse.

Now would be the time to reflect on the redemptive implications of Jesus' crucifixion. Jesus took our place on the cross and atoned for our sins. Maybe you can relate to the substitution Jesus made. When you were sexually abused as a child you may have been taking the place of another child, a sibling or a child in your neighborhood. You may consider returning to your memories and accepting your abuse as your act of self-sacrificial love on behalf of other children who would have been abused otherwise. You are on the path to spiritually healing from the abuse, and you will survive. Not everyone who is abused will be as fortunate. Making the sacrifice retrospectively in your mind does not make it any less noble.

XI

Eleventh Station

Jesus is nailed to the Cross

We adore you, O Christ, and we bless you:
Because by your holy cross you have redeemed the world.

When they came to the place which is called The Skull,
there they crucified him; and with him they crucified two
criminals, one on the right, the other on the left, and Jesus
between them. And the scripture was fulfilled which says,
"He was numbered with the transgressors."

V. They pierce my hands and my feet:
R. They stare and gloat over me.

Let us pray. *(Silence)*

Lord Jesus Christ, you stretched out your arms of love on
the hard wood of the cross that everyone might come
within the reach of your saving embrace: So clothe us in
your Spirit that we, reaching forth our hands in love, may
bring those who do not know you to the knowledge and
love of you; for the honor of your Name. *Amen.*

Holy God,
Holy and Mighty,
Holy Immortal One,
Have mercy upon us.

Reflection

At the Eleventh Station, Jesus is nailed to the cross. Use this time of nonresistance as you reflect upon your abuse to apply what you learned when working Stations 4-7 and evaluate which social factors contributed to your abuse in each instance of the abuse that you can remember.

Jesus was numbered with the transgressors; his accusers reduced him to the status of a criminal, deserving of death. How did the low value that your abuser assigned to human life contribute to your abuse? Now is the time to give back to your abuser(s) any negative feelings you internalized about yourself from their mistreatment of you and remind yourself that as a child of God you deserve love and respect, just like everyone else.

Knowing what you know now about the various factors which contributed to your abuse, you can serve as your own fair witness of what occurred. No longer are you in the role of Pilate as you were at the First Station, you are now in the role of Jesus; you know the facts. Surrendering to the facts surrounding your abuse and allowing yourself to feel the feelings associated with various aspects of your abuse will free you from the victim role, if you choose to be liberated. Some survivors remain trapped in the victim role and go on to be victimized by others their entire lives, surrendering their power and preferences to anyone who asks, oblivious of their feelings and desires. You now have the power to take control of your life. Use that power. God holds us accountable for our actions (Matthew 25:14-30). It is your responsibility to care for yourself and make good use of the talents and resources God has entrusted to you. Remember the love you found for yourself at the Fourth Station? Reflect on that love and consider how it can be mobilized to assist you in meeting those obligations.

XII

Twelfth Station

Jesus dies on the Cross

We adore you, O Christ, and we bless you:
Because by your holy cross you have redeemed the world.

When Jesus saw his mother, and the disciple whom he loved standing near, he said to his mother, "Woman, behold your son!" Then he said to the disciple, "Behold your mother!" And when Jesus had received the vinegar, he said, "It is finished!" And then, crying with a loud voice, he said, "Father, into your hands I commend my spirit." And he bowed his head, and handed over his spirit.

V. Christ for us became obedient unto death:
R. Even death on a cross.

Let us pray. *(Silence)*

O God, who for our redemption gave your only-begotten Son to the death of the cross, and by his glorious resurrection delivered us from the power of our enemy: Grant us so to die daily to sin, that we may evermore live with him in the joy of his resurrection; who lives and reigns now and for ever. *Amen.*

Holy God,
Holy and Mighty,
Holy Immortal One,
Have mercy upon us.

Reflection

Prior to Jesus' death he forms a new family by joining his mother and the disciple whom he loves as mother and son. Hopefully by reviewing your abuse in the context of the Stations of the Cross you have managed to unify your adult self with the trembling, frightened child you were at the time of the abuse. Use this friendship to your advantage to heal from the abuse. Resolve to care for yourself in the manner in which you were not cared for as a child. Seek help to resolve difficulties with intimacy or self-esteem that carried over from the abuse into your adult life. Just as Jesus' suffering was finished at the cross, our suffering and fear can be left at the Twelfth Station, at the foot of the cross, and spiritually liberated from the contemplation of our abuse, we can move on to discover God's other plans for our life.

For I know the plans I have for you, says the LORD, plans for welfare and not for evil, to give you a future and a hope.

– Jeremiah 29:11, RSV Bible

XIII

Thirteenth Station

The body of Jesus is placed in the arms of his mother

We adore you, O Christ, and we bless you:
Because by your holy cross you have redeemed the world.

All you who pass by, behold and see if there is any sorrow like my sorrow. My eyes are spent with weeping; my soul is in tumult; my heart is poured out in grief because of the downfall of my people. "Do not call me Naomi (which means Pleasant), call me Mara (which means Bitter); for the Almighty has dealt very bitterly with me."

V. Her tears run down her cheeks:
R. And she has none to comfort her.

Let us pray. *(Silence)*

Lord Jesus Christ, by your death you took away the sting of death: Grant to us your servants so to follow in faith where you have led the way, that we may at length fall asleep peacefully in you and wake up in your likeness; for your tender mercies' sake. *Amen.*

Holy God,
Holy and Mighty,
Holy Immortal One,
Have mercy upon us.

Reflection

Reflecting on our memories of childhood sexual abuse can sharpen our awareness of the extent to which our abuse has negatively impacted our life. This can be a cause for grief. Give yourself permission to mourn lost relationships, missed opportunities, and the compromised quality of life that may have resulted from the residual symptoms you experience as an abuse survivor or from the erroneous beliefs that you have held. You may find that grieving frees up your energy to focus on healing from residual symptoms, but be aware that grief, in and of itself, is a healing process. Let it run its course.

XIV

Fourteenth Station

Jesus is laid in the tomb

We adore you, O Christ, and we bless you:
Because by your holy cross you have redeemed the world.

When it was evening, there came a rich man from
Arimathea, named Joseph, who also was a disciple of Jesus.
He went to Pilate and asked for the body of Jesus. Then
Pilate ordered it to be given to him. And Joseph took the
body, and wrapped it in a clean linen shroud, and laid it in
his own new tomb, which he had hewn in the rock; and he
rolled a great stone to the door of the tomb.

V. You will not abandon me to the grave:
R. Nor let your holy One see corruption.

Let us pray. *(Silence)*

O God, your blessed Son was laid in a tomb in a garden,
and rested on the Sabbath day: Grant that we who have
been buried with him in the waters of baptism may find our
perfect rest in his eternal and glorious kingdom; where he
lives and reigns for ever and ever. *Amen.*

Holy God,
Holy and Mighty,
Holy Immortal One,
Have mercy upon us.

Reflection

The Fourteenth Station challenges us to have faith in the healing process. Like Joseph of Arimathea when he committed Jesus' body to the tomb, we commit our wounded self to the care of God. Do so in the faith that you will be healed, and as often as you doubt it return to the Fourteenth station and remember that God will do with your body what he did on Easter morning with Jesus', if not in this life than in the next. Spiritually, your healing is already well under way, and the new life God intended for you from the creation of the world, your life in Christ, is already being revealed. Embrace that life and you will find meaning and happiness beyond your wildest dreams.

The Altar

Concluding Prayers before the Altar

Savior of the world, by your cross and precious blood you
have redeemed us:
Save us, and help us, we humbly beseech you, O Lord.

Let us pray. *(Silence)*

We thank you, heavenly Father, that you have delivered us
from the dominion of sin and death and brought us into the
kingdom of your Son; and we pray that, as by his death he
has recalled us to life, so by his love he may raise us to
eternal joys; who lives and reigns with you, in the unity of
the Holy Spirit, one God, now and for ever. *Amen.*

To Christ our Lord who loves us, and washed us in his own
blood, and made us a kingdom of priests to serve his God
and Father, to him be glory and dominion for ever and ever.
Amen.

www.ingramcontent.com/pod-product-compliance
Lightning Source LLC
Chambersburg PA
CBHW031334040426
42443CB00005B/342